A Family's Story

Jeanne Dustman M.A.Ed.

Consultants

Sharon Coan, M.S.Ed.
Strategic Planning Executive
Teacher Created Materials

Shelley Scudder
Gifted Education Teacher
Broward County Schools

Caryn Williams, M.S.Ed.
Madison County Schools
Huntsville, AL

Publishing Credits

Conni Medina, M.A.Ed., *Managing Editor*
Lee Aucoin, *Creative Director*
Torrey Maloof, *Editor*
Marissa Rodriguez, *Designer*
Stephanie Reid, *Photo Editor*
Rachelle Cracchiolo, M.S.Ed., *Publisher*

Image Credits: Cover, back cover, pp. 1, 4 (left & right), 6, 7, 8, 10, 12, 18, 22, 23, 24, 25, 26, 27, 28, (left & right), 29 (top & bottom) Sharon Coan; p.5 The Granger Collection; p. 3 BigStock; pp. 12–13, 15, 21 Getty Images; p. 20 , 32 The Library of Congress [LC-USF33-016126-M1]; p. 16 The Library of Congress [LC-USF34-073917-D]; All other images from Shutterstock.

Teacher Created Materials
5301 Oceanus Drive
Huntington Beach, CA 92649-1030
http://www.tcmpub.com

ISBN 978-1-4333-6992-6

Printed in China
Nordica.012019.CA21801581

Table of Contents

Morrie

Winnie

In the Beginning

This is a story about Sharon's family. The story begins with her parents. They are named Morrie and Winnie. They met in 1929 in a one-room school in Sycamore (SIK-uh-mawr), Illinois (il-uh-NOI).

Room for School

Long ago, schools only had one large room. In that room, there would be eight grades. One teacher taught all the grades.

Morrie was in sixth grade. Winnie was in first grade. They both lived on farms. Morrie pulled Winnie's pigtails. He said that he would marry her someday.

Winnie and Morrie were married in 1941. Morrie worked for the railroad. Winnie took care of their home. Soon, Sharon was born. Later, her sister and two brothers were born.

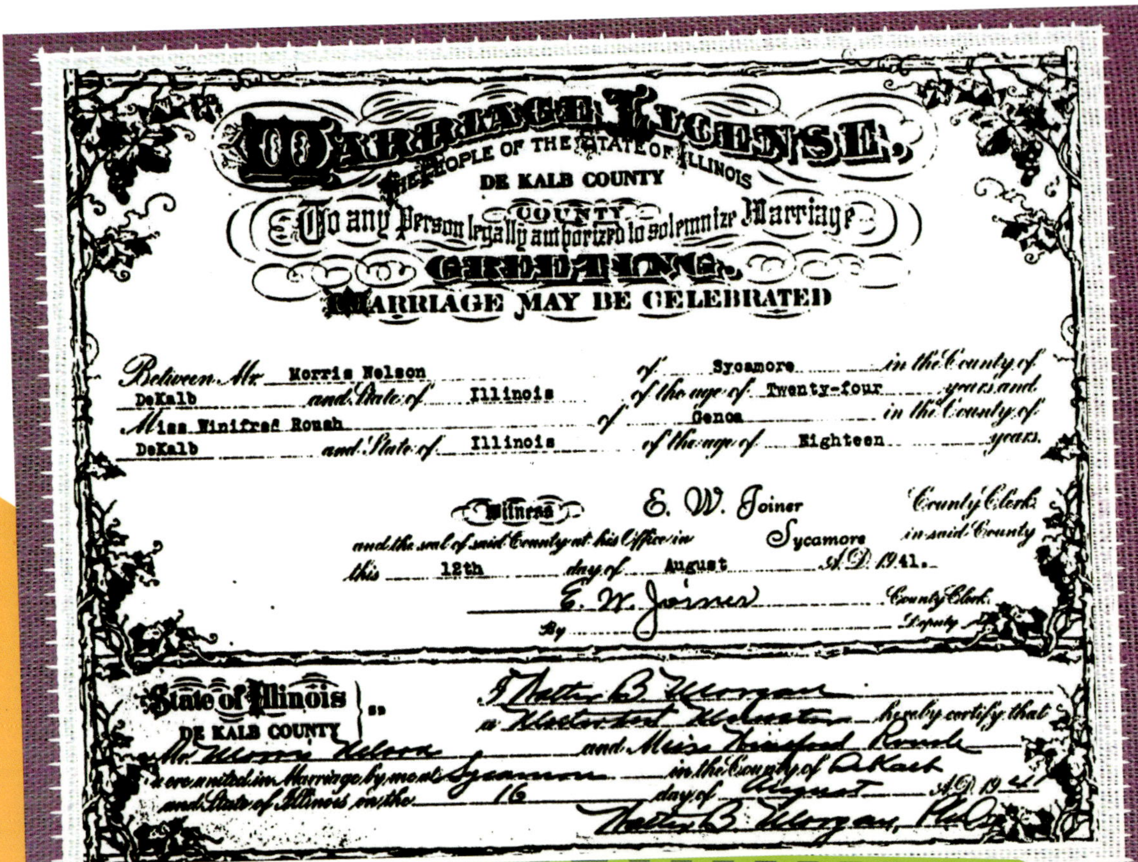

MARRIAGE LICENSE,
THE PEOPLE OF THE STATE OF ILLINOIS
DE KALB COUNTY
To any Person legally authorized to solemnize Marriage
GREETING:
MARRIAGE MAY BE CELEBRATED

Between Mr. Morris Nelson of Sycamore in the County of DeKalb and State of Illinois of the age of Twenty-four years and Miss Winifred Roush of Genoa in the County of DeKalb and State of Illinois of the age of Eighteen years.

Witness E. W. Joiner County Clerk and the seal of said County at his Office in Sycamore in said County this 12th day of August A.D. 1941.

E. W. Joiner County Clerk.
By Deputy

State of Illinois } ss.
DE KALB COUNTY

Walter B. Morgan a Methodist Minister hereby certify that Mr. Morris Nelson and Miss Winifred Roush were united in Marriage by me at Sycamore in the County of DeKalb and State of Illinois on the 16 day of August A.D. 1941

Walter B. Morgan, Ph.D.

This paper shows that Sharon's parents were married.

Sharon's father loved his kids. He liked to take them to the railroad station to see the **soldiers** (SOHL-jerz). The soldiers were coming home from **World War II**. They threw coins and candy to the kids.

This is Sharon as a baby.

Country Life

Sharon's family moved to an old farmhouse. Sharon was four years old.

Sharon's family lived in this farmhouse.

At first, their farmhouse did not have indoor **plumbing** (PLUHM-ing). Plumbing is a system of pipes. The pipes carry water through a house. Sharon's family had to use an outdoor bathroom called an *outhouse*. Later, they put in plumbing. They made an indoor bathroom.

Outdoor Business

Long ago, families had outhouses instead of bathrooms. Outhouses were cold and dark at night.

When Sharon was eight, one more sister was born. The five kids loved to play outside. They loved to explore the land around their house.

Sharon (top left) is posing with her brothers and sisters.

Sharon liked to play under a big weeping willow tree. She chased fireflies at night. Fireflies are bugs that light up in the dark.

Time to Play!

Back then, kids played outside more often. Some of the most popular games were tag, hide-and-seek, and hopscotch.

This is a weeping willow tree like the one Sharon played under.

Sharon and her family lived in a **rural** (ROOR-uhl) area. She did not live in the city. She and her brothers and sisters went to school in town. They had to walk a long way to the school bus stop.

Sharon is ready to walk to the bus stop.

The bus ride to and from the school was also long. The kids were very tired when they got home.

Sharon rode a school bus like this one.

Hard Work

When Sharon was young, her mother had a big garden. Sharon's mother grew fruits and vegetables. She stored them in jars. She used them to make pies.

Sharon's mother made apple pies like this one.

The whole family helped in the garden. They liked to pick the **ripe** fruits and vegetables. Keeping up the garden was hard work. But the food was healthy and good to eat!

Sharon's mother had a garden just like this one.

This woman is milking a cow.

Sharon's family took care of animals, too. They had chickens and two cows. They got eggs from the chickens. They got milk from the cows.

Sharon's family had small pigs like these.

Sharon's uncle gave them small pigs. Her mother cared for the tiny pigs. The pigs became pets. They also had dogs. Sharon's favorite dog was named Tippy.

Celebrations and Traditions

Sharon's family did not work all the time. They liked to party, too! Her family had many **celebrations** (sel-uh-BREY-shuhnz) when she was young. Celebrations are parties for special days. Sharon loved Christmas the most.

This is Sharon (front left) and her family in 1949.

Each year, they had a Christmas tree. There were gifts. There was love. The whole family would get together. One year, there were 52 people together for Christmas!

Sharon's family had a Christmas tree like this one.

Sharon's family enjoyed picnics like this one.

Traditions (truh-DISH-uhnz) are ways of doing things that have been done by a family for a long time. Sharon's family had many traditions. They loved to go for Sunday drives. They took picnic lunches with them.

Sharon's family bought ice cream from a market like this one.

On the way home, they would go to Brown's Corner Market. Sharon's father would ask her mother if they should buy some I.C. The kids would get excited. They knew *I.C.* meant "ice cream"!

City Life

In 1954, Sharon's family moved to West Chicago (shi-KAH-go). She was 12 years old. It was a big change to leave their home in the country. Now, they lived in a town near a big city.

This is Sharon graduating from college.

When she grew up, Sharon went to college and became a teacher. Then, Sharon met a man named Don. They fell in love and were married in 1968.

Sharon and Don cut their wedding cake.

Her Own Family

Soon, Sharon and Don had their own family. They had two girls named Dara and Tami. They were a busy family. They liked to take many trips. The trips reminded Sharon of her family's Sunday drives.

Sharon stands with her family on a trip to Washington, DC.

Sharon's girls liked to do many things. Dara liked to dance. Tami liked to sing. Both girls were in Girl Scouts. Sharon was their **troop** leader.

This is Dara dancing.

Over the years, Sharon's family grew up. Her girls went to college. Then, Dara married a man named Pete. They had a baby girl in 2009. They named her Hana. Sharon spends as much time with Hana as she can.

This is Dara and Pete.

Today, Sharon and Don like to travel. They like to spend time with their family and watch it grow. Sharon loves her family very much.

This is Sharon with Dara and Hana.

Tell It!

Sharon and her family have a story. Your family has a story, too! Draw or write the story of your family. Share your story with a friend.

This is Sharon as a baby.

This is Don and Sharon.

This is Sharon cooking with her family.

This is Sharon and her family.

Glossary

celebrations—special or fun things people do for an important event or holiday

plumbing—pipes that carry water through a building

ripe—fully grown and ready to be eaten

rural—relating to the country, instead of the city

soldiers—people who are in the military

traditions—ways of thinking or doing things that have been used by a group of people or a family for a long time

troop—a group of people

World War II—a war between many countries, from 1939–1945

Index

Your Turn!

Family Traditions

Sharon's family had a tradition of taking Sunday drives. Sometimes, they would stop for a picnic or ice cream.

Does your family have any traditions? Make a list of all the traditions that your family enjoys.